Holistic Homemaking:
Guide to Reducing Toxic Exposure and Creating Natural Products

The information in this book is not intended to give or replace medical care, advice or provide treatment of any condition. Do not start or stop any holistic remedy without first contacting your healthcare provider.

All rights reserved. Copyright: Author Winslow E. Dixon.

No part of this publication may be reproduced, distributed, or transmitted in any form or by any means, including photocopying, recording, or other electronic or mechanical methods, without the prior written permission of the publisher, except in the case of brief quotations embodied in critical reviews and certain other noncommercial uses permitted by copyright law. For permission requests, please contact the author.

ISBN: 9781734907322

Library of Congress Control Number: 2021907706

Printed in the United States of America.

First printing edition 2021

For more information on holistic homemaking visit the website: hopehealinghappy.com

Chapter 1: Concerning Chemicals 5
Toxic Exposure 6
Formula for Identifying Toxins 7
Candles: Comforting or Cancerous? 9
Is Citric Acid Natural? 10
Are Laundry Products Safe? 10
Is Nail Polish Toxic? 13
Is Deodorant Dangerous? 14

Chapter 2: Holistic Homemaking Supplies 17
Activated Charcoal 17
Aloe Vera 18
Baking soda 18
Beeswax 20
Bentonite Clay 22
Body butters 22
Borax 23
Carrier oil 23
Castile soap 24
Castor oil 24
Epsom salt 24
Essential Oils 25
Felts Naptha 26
Glycerin 27
Kosher salt 27
Mica 27
Neem 28
Unflavored gelatin 28
White Vinegar 28
Witch Hazel 29

Chapter 3: Holistic Homemaking Recipes 29
Air Freshener Spray 29
Bathroom Cleaner 30
Dishwasher Pods 31
Disinfectant Spray 32

Floor Cleaner 33
Furniture Polish 34
Gel Air Freshener 35
Glass Cleaner 36
Laundry Detergent 37
Surface Disinfectant Wipes 38

Chapter 4: Personal Hygiene Recipes 39
Acne Cleansing Mask 39
Acne Astringent 40
Moisturizing Conditioner 41
Holistic Shampoo 42
Skin Disinfectant Wipes 43
Tooth Whitening Paste 44

Chapter 5: Miscellaneous Recipes 45
Ant Repellent 45
Anti-Flea Shampoo 46
Baby Wipes 47
Bug Repellent 48
Eye Serum 49
Jelly Soap 50
Mascara 51
Pet Calming Spray 52
Sleepy Time Salve 53
Weedkiller 54

Chapter 6: First Aid Kit 55
Antiseptic Spray 55
Congestion Relief Rub 56
Pain Relief Rub 57
Restless Leg Relief Rub 58
Stretch Mark Salve 59
Sunscreen 60
Natural Neosporin 61

Chapter 7: Comfort Products 62
Anti-Anxiety Calming Wipe Recipe 62
Bath Bombs *Citric Acid Free* 63
Lemon Shea Butter 64
Spiced Apple Body Butter 65

Chapter 8: Conclusion 66
References 67
Acknowledgements 68
About the Author 69

Chapter 1: Concerning Chemicals

The question of whether organic products are necessary or not is a current topic in today's world. Are the chemicals in household cleaning supplies, makeup and beauty products really toxic to you and your family's health? The Environmental Policy and Children's Health Association states that[1], "Children have chemical exposures from birth that their parents didn't have until they were adults. Because children are exposed to toxins at an earlier age than adults, they have more time to develop environmentally triggered diseases, with long latency periods, such as cancer."

Knowing this information, it is no wonder why families are searching for natural, organic options to replace the harsh chemicals used in household products. The awareness regarding toxic exposure is an important step towards protecting our health from toxins.

The United States House of Representatives Report in 1989 published some alarming statistics regarding the toxicity that American's are regularly exposed to. "Of the chemicals found in personal care products: 884 are toxic, 146 cause tumors, 218 cause reproductive complications, 778 cause acute toxicity, 314 cause biological mutations, 376 cause skin and eye irritations."

Americans are unknowingly exposed to more toxins in the current day and age than ever before. Perhaps this is why

---

[1] Landrigan PJ, Carlson JE. Environmental policy and children's health. Future Child. 1995 Summer-Fall;5(2):34-52. PMID: 8528687.

cancer, autoimmune disease and allergic reactions are increasing at an alarming rate?

To find our best health possible, it is imperative we reduce our exposure to environmental toxins. Despite the alarming statistics of chemical toxicity in the current age, there is good news, you can take control of your chemical exposure! Natural, organic products can be used to replace the toxin filled products in your home. A great way to do this is to swap out toxic products with safe, effective replacements. You can use a variety of natural ingredients to create organic items which are safe for you and your family. This book is a guide on how to identify and eliminate toxic exposure in your life and how to replace them with safe, holistic solutions. This practice is referred to as "holistic homemaking."

Toxic Exposure

Chemicals are especially present in products used in our homes such as cleaning supplies, laundry detergents, make-up and even in our foods and beverages. For example, Parabens and phthalates are commonly used chemicals which have been researched to cause cancer and type II diabetes. These two chemicals can be found in shampoo, make-up and various beauty products. Aluminum is also a common additive used in antiperspirants and scented products despite the fact that this toxin has been linked to increasing the risks of developing Alzheimer's disease and breast cancer.

To live the most optimal life possible, limiting your exposure your toxins is essential to your wellbeing. Many people are unaware at how many subtle chemicals we are exposed to through modern conveniences such as household cleaners, detergents and dishwashing liquid.

Learning to identify toxins in household products, cleaning supplies, makeup and personal hygiene products is essential to finding optimal health possible. But how can you know which ones are safe and which ones are potentially dangerous?

Formula for Eliminating Toxins

- Read
- Research
- Replace

The first step is to read every label of every product that you purchase. It is important to know what the chemical composition is of products that go into your body, on your skin and are used in your home, car or office.

The second step is to research the ingredients found in the products. Odds are, if an ingredient has been banned in another country or has negative research about it you will be able to find this information online.

The third step is to replace concerning products with natural, nontoxic solutions.

Traditional products can contain the following concerning chemicals:

Phthalates are ingredients used in many cosmetics and other products to soften solvents. These chemicals have shown the possibility of damaging human health.

Parabens are a type of preservative used in many beauty and skincare products. The danger with these chemicals is that they can mimic estrogen in the body. When applied to the skin, they can seep into the bloodstream and create hormone imbalances and disrupt the body's homeostasis.

SLS (sodium lauryl sulfate)/SLES (sodium laureth sulfate)

This ingredient is what makes detergent lather and causes it to clean through grease. This chemical absorbs into the skin and has been known to cause rashes and allergic reactions.

DEA (diethanolamine), MEA (monoethanolamine), TEA (triethanolamine)

These chemicals have been shown to disrupt hormones in the human body and are known for creating nitrates and nitrosamines. They also increased your risk of developing 1,4-dioxane toxicity due to regular exposure to these types of chemicals.

Triclosan

This chemical is a standard ingredient in traditional soaps because it acts as an antibacterial, anti-fungal and antiviral. It can be a hazard because it can disrupt the endocrine system and is a known "endocrine disruptor."

Fragrance

The FDA does not mandate that chemicals listed as "fragrance" must be revealed on labeling or disclosed to consumers. Any given fragrance mixture can contain up to 3,000 chemicals.

Candles: Comforting or Cancer Causing?

Candles are a staple of relaxing comfort in most American homes, but most people would be alarmed to discover that candles can be toxic and harmful to their health. Candles can contain chemicals which are known to damage the human body and cause cancer. Exposure to these chemicals have also been linked to lung and central nervous system damage and have been a precursor to developmental difficulties in children.

The University of Michigan released a study[2] that revealed 30% of candles contained lead. When lit, these candles emit toxins into the air and we inhale them. Our lungs can easily become damaged when exposed to lead, so the safety of lead containing candles is definitely questionable.

Paraffin is another common candle ingredient which is toxic. It is a waste product created from petroleum, and yet it is placed into candles and sold despite its negative effects. When heated, paraffin releases a carcinogenic chemical in the air. The Occupational Safety and Health Administration (OSHA) reports that, "Pure paraffin wax is widely regarded as non-toxic, but may possess some carcinogenic properties." (Source: OSHA- Ref 5.3)

The Safe Drinking Water and Toxic Enforcement Act of 1986 passed in the State of California revealed that there are at least seven major toxins in paraffin wax. Paraffin

---

[2] Some candles with lead wicks emit lead into the air. (n.d.). University of Michigan News and Information Services http://ns.umich.edu/Releases/1999/Oct99/r100699.html

wax falls into the category of toxic chemicals known as petrochemicals, which are byproducts derived from petroleum. Yes! Petroleum, which includes fuels such as gasoline, kerosene, and diesel oil. So essentially, when you are lighting a paraffin wax candle you are allowing gasoline-like toxins to enter the air in your home.

Is citric acid really natural?

In the current age, most citric acid is not made from lemons. It is derived from mold. Citric acid is derived from aspergillus niger, which is a form of black mold. Commercially produced citric acid is made by manipulating sugars exposed to black mold and filtered using sulfuric acid, which is a genetically modified organism (GMO). Citric acid was formerly made from fruit, but corporations found a cheaper short-cut by producing the GMO form. Unfortunately, this is now the common practice. GMO derived citric acid is a common ingredient, food additive, and preservative which can trigger allergic reactions in those who are sensitive to it.

Are laundry products safe?

Many of us don't think twice before throwing a couple of dryer sheets in with a clean load of laundry. After all, they cause our clothes to have a fresh scent and can cut down on static cling. But are we unknowingly exposing ourselves to chemicals? What do household cleaning products really contain?

There is no law in the United States that requires products of any kind to list chemicals used in fragrances. However, the University of Washington enacted a study that tested the ingredients of multiple laundry detergent brands. Their study[3] revealed dangerous chemicals such as: Acetone, an active ingredient in paint thinner; chloromethane which was once widely used as a refrigerant but due to its toxicity is no longer used as such. 1,4-dioxane was also discovered. The EPA reports that exposure to 1,4-Dioxane [4] can cause, "Acute (short-term) inhalation exposure to high levels of 1,4-dioxane has caused vertigo, drowsiness, headache, anorexia, and irritation of the eyes, nose, throat, and lungs in humans. Damage to the liver and kidneys has been observed in rats chronically (long-term) exposed in their drinking water. Tumors have been observed in orally exposed animals. EPA has classified 1,4-dioxane as a Group B2, probable human carcinogen."

Phthalates, which are defined as chemicals used to soften and increase the flexibility of plastic and vinyl, were also found in laundry detergent.

The Food and Drug Administration requires all American food distributors to list all ingredients, and yet there is no law that requires laundry products to list chemicals used in fragrances.

The Consumer Product Safety Commission does not require manufacturers to list all ingredients on the label. This is concerning because without a true understanding of what chemicals a product contains, you cannot truly assess whether it is a health hazard or not.

---

[3] University of Washington. (2010, October 28). Scented consumer products shown to emit many unlisted chemicals. https://www.washington.edu/news/2010/10/28/scented-consumer-products-shown-to-emit-many-unlisted-chemicals-3/
[4] Environmental Protection Agency. (n.d.). 1,4-Dioxane (1,4-Diethyleneoxide). Retrieved from https://www.epa.gov/assessing-and-managing-chemicals-under-tsca/risk-evaluation-14-dioxane

Researchers at the University of Washington, led by Dr. Anne Steinemann, a professor of civil and environmental engineering and public affairs, expounded research to discover the chemical composition of many household products. They conducted a study that examined laundry detergents, dryer sheets, soaps, air fresheners, aerosol disinfectants and many other household products from a wide variety of companies.

The study[5] revealed the following shocking results:

1- Every single product which was tested emitted at least one chemical classified as toxic or hazardous.

2-11 of the tested products emitted at least one probable carcinogen according to the EPA.

3-Some of the tested products contained the following hazardous chemicals: Acetaldehyde, 1,4-dioxane, Formaldehyde and Methylene Chloride.

4- In total, the tested products emitted more than 420 chemicals. The majority of these chemicals were not listed on the label or disclosed to consumers.

5-The majority of products contained acetone and ethanol, which are chemicals found in nail polish remover.

Dr. Steinemann's further research studies discovered 10 percent of subjects surveyed complained of negative effects from laundry products. Patients surveyed with asthma were also reported to have increased symptoms when exposed to

---

[5] U. (2010, October 28). Scented consumer products shown to emit many unlisted chemicals.
https://www.washington.edu/news/2010/10/28/scented-consumer-products-shown-to-emit-many-unlisted-chemicals-3/

certain household products, especially those containing fragrances.

Knowing this information, avoiding as many toxic chemicals as possible is obviously a good decision for your health. Fortunately, there are safe, natural alternatives to store bought household products if you so choose to give them up.

Is Nail Polish toxic?

A fresh manicure is one of the best ways to practice pampering and self-care, but did you know that some of the ingredients in nail polish can be possibly toxic to your health?

A research study[6] performed by Duke University revealed that the majority of nail polish products contained hormone-disrupting chemicals that are indeed health hazards such as Triphenyl phosphate (TPHP) which is a chemical used as a flame retardant. It is also concerning that most nail hardening products contain formaldehyde, which is a known toxin. Because of this, the FDA has issued a limit on the amount of formaldehyde allowed in nail care and beauty products. But the argument is that any exposure, even in small amounts is not the best choice for anyone's health.

Currently, there are no American laws that require cosmetic companies to report complaints to the FDA. If certain nail polish brands are causing health concerns, the public may not be made aware of it.

---

[6] Environment International, Volume 86, 2016, Pages 45-51, ISSN 0160-4120

Concerning ingredients which may be in nail polish products:

Acetyl triethyl citrate
Butyl alcohol
Benzene
Benzophenones
Camphor
Ferric ammonium ferrocyanide.
Ethyl tosylamide
FD&C and D&C colors
Formaldehyde
Toluene sulfonamide
Nanoparticle titanium dioxide (and other nanoparticles)
Xylene

Fortunately, there are nail polish companies that offer non-toxic nail care options. It is important to fully research the ingredients in any product you are going to put on or in your body.

Is Deodorant Dangerous?

Putting on deodorant is a normal part of our hygiene routines. It helps keep us smelling fresh and clean, but did you know that this common practice may be harming your health?

What concerning ingredients can deodorant contain?

Aluminum chlorohydrate is one of the most common compounds used in antiperspirants. It is included in up to 25% of hygiene products and is typically added as an antiperspirant. Aluminum salts plug sweat proteins that bind to the wall of the sweat duct, thus having an anti-sweating effect.

Triclosan is a compound shown to impact the body's hormones and can interfere with hormonal signaling. Triclosan's endocrine disrupting factors have been proven by a myriad of scientific studies [7] and because of this, the FDA actually banned its use in hand soaps. It is still permitted in low amounts in items such as deodorant.

Diethanolamine[8] **(DEA)** is a compound used in deodorant and other hygiene products that has been linked to increased risks of developing cancer.

Parabens are chemicals used in traditional care products that mimic estrogen's role in the body. Parabens have been linked [9] to the development of breast cancer.

How does deodorant impact the body?

When the above chemicals are applied to the skin, they are absorbed and can spread into tissues and even organ systems, causing possible disruption and may contribute to health issues and elevate cancer risks.

---

[7] James MO, Li W, Summerlot DP, Rowland-Faux L, Wood CE. Triclosan is a potent inhibitor of estradiol and estrone sulfonation in sheep placenta. Environ Int. 2010 Nov;36(8):942-9. doi: 10.1016/j.envint.2009.02.004. Epub 2009 Mar 18. PMID: 19299018; PMCID: PMC4789100.

[8] *Diethanolamine* [Https://monographs.iarc.who.int/wp-content/uploads/2018/06/mono101-004.pdf]. (n.d.).

[9] Breast Cancer Prevention Partners. (n.d.). Parabens. Retrieved from https://www.bcpp.org/resource/parabens/

Research[10] shows that aluminum chlorohydrate, when applied to the skin showed 0.012% of the applied aluminum was absorbed through the skin, which accounted for 4 mcg of aluminum being absorbed following a single application. Aluminum has been linked to a wide range of health issues, including Alzheimer's and dementia.

Antiperspirants are also not recommended because the body has processes it uses to detoxify itself. Sweating is the body's way of ridding itself of toxins and when you inhibit your body's ability to remove contaminants, you do not expel toxins your body needs to get rid of. Sweating is a natural process that must be done in order to have the most optimal health possible.

Why take the chance of unknown chemicals being added into your home and onto your body when you can create natural products instead?

Chapter 2: Making Natural Products

Making your own natural products can be a great way to take control of your toxic exposure and help you live a healthier lifestyle, but only if done safely and effectively. When making your own products, be sure to use only 100% pure, organic products that have been verified for purity standards by organizations such as the USDA.

Additionally, the containers you put your products into are just as important as the products themselves. You want to be sure you are using safe, heat resistant containers that are free from toxins such as BPA, which is an industrial

---

[10] Drug Bank (n.d.). Aluminum chlorohydrate. Retrieved from https://go.drugbank.com/drugs/DB11573

chemical found in polycarbonate plastics, epoxy resins and disposable water bottles.

This chapter will highlight the most commonly used ingredients for making alternative products. Be sure you are researching the brands you choose to buy and always speak with your doctor before starting any holistic remedy.

Holistic Product Bases

Activated Charcoal

When most people hear of charcoal, they think of the black, rock like substance used at cookouts to start grill fires. But did you know there is another form of charcoal that has many health benefits? Activated charcoal can be formed from bamboo, wood or olive pits but is mainly created from coconut shells. The process of creating activated charcoal happens when the char substance is heated to a high temperature. These high temperatures change the chemical structure of the char substance, increasing the surface area and "activating" the charcoal. This form of charcoal can be used to provide many health benefits. Activated charcoal has a negative electrical charge which causes it to attract toxins and gases. This form of charcoal is non-toxic and cannot be absorbed by the human body, which allows it to freely carry the toxins out of the body through the feces.

Do not ingest any substance without first checking with your healthcare provider.

Aloe Vera

Aloe vera has been used for thousands of years as a natural healing remedy. In ancient Egypt, it was referred to as the "plant of immortality." In the current age, people can still find a myriad of benefits from using aloe. Aloe is a natural treatment for sunburns and has been clinically proven to reduce the damage from ultraviolent rays and radiation. A natural, aloe vera salve can be applied to sunburned areas to soothe the skin and help prevent UV damage. As a naturally hydrating substance, aloe can be taken internally to keep your body hydrated. When taking a natural substance internally, it is important to choose a high-quality product. Many aloe juices on the market are not 100% pure and are mixed with other contents. Be sure you are reading the label of the product you are purchasing and do not start any alternative treatment without first checking with your physician. Certain medications may interact with aloe juice, so be sure that you make your healthcare team aware of any medications and supplements you are taking before you begin an aloe juice regiment. Aloe vera contains many nutritional benefits such as calcium, copper, chromium, sodium, selenium, magnesium, potassium, manganese, and zinc. It is also one of the only natural, plant-based sources of vitamin b12, which can benefit those who eat a vegan or meatless diet.

Baking soda

Baking soda is an inexpensive, natural product with a wide array of uses. Baking soda, also known as sodium bicarbonate, is a white powdery substance known for its many household uses. Baking soda can also be used in ways other than just making cookies and keeping your refrigerator smelling fresh.

Possible Benefits of Baking Soda:

- **Alkalinizing Agent.** For optimal health, the body needs to maintain a state of alkalinity, which means that the PH balance must not be to acidic or to alkaline. Baking soda is a naturally alkalinizing compound and can help your body reduce acidity.

- **Athletic Performance Booster.** Many studies have shown that endurance athletes who ingest sodium bicarbonate report that baking soda improves their endurance and lessens fatigue after training and work out sessions.

- **Anti-Acid Treatment.** As a naturally alkalinizing agent, baking soda is an old holistic remedy for treating acid reflux and also has shown it can help gas pressure and bloating.

- **Produce Cleanser.** Dirt, pesticides, and other contaminants need to be cleaned off of your produce before you can ingest them safely. Soaking your fruits and vegetables in a solution of baking soda and warm water will help remove toxins.

- **Household Cleaner.** Chemicals such as bleach and ammonia can exacerbate health issues and irritate the eyes and skin. Replacing these toxic items with a baking soda solution is a great natural way to clean your home.

- **Laundry Booster.** Sprinkling a ½ cup of baking soda into your load of laundry will add a natural boost of freshness and cleansing to even the dirtiest of clothing.

Beeswax

Beeswax is a substance produced by worker bees, which is secreted by glands on the bee's abdomen. It is naturally a yellow-brownish color, but can also be purified to different shades of yellow or even white. Beeswax has been used since ancient times for its amazing benefits. Ancient Egyptians and Roman cultures used beeswax for natural skin and beauty treatments. Today, it is still used in the production of many products such as candles, lotions, and cosmetic products.

Beeswax has a variety of uses such as:

- **Natural Base for homemade products**. Beeswax is a wonderful component to add to your life if you are a DIY enthusiast. Natural products such as candles, chapsticks, makeup and lotions can be made without the use of chemicals and toxins.

- **Acne Treatment**. Due to its rich vitamin A content and anti-septic properties, beeswax is an amazing natural treatment for acne. It moisturizes the skin without clogging pores and allows skin to "breathe."

- **Anti-inflammatory**. Beeswax has been researched to help ease inflammation and joint pain in patients with arthritis and joint stiffness/pain. It is an added ingredient in many topical creams to ease pain and discomfort.

- **Skin Care**. Beeswax contains vitamin A and is moisturizing to skin yet does not clog pores. It is also used in the treatment of skin conditions such as eczema, diaper rash, dermatitis, and psoriasis. Beeswax has been researched to help the body produce collagen which can aid in the healing of stretch marks and scars.

What is the difference between white and yellow beeswax?

White and yellow beeswax pellets differ in color based on the filtration process. White beeswax is turned white after undergoing a pressure-filtration process. Yellow beeswax is typically processed less and therefore left in its more natural state.

Which Beeswax should you use?

Choosing the right beeswax product is dependent on what you are using the beeswax for. It is important to choose a pure, 100% organic natural beeswax product that does not contain other filler ingredients. Be sure you research the quality of the beeswax you are purchasing.

- **White beeswax** is great for projects such as candle making because you can create lots of different colored candles with natural mica powder. Beeswax candles are naturally hypoallergenic and emit negative ions into the air, which have various health benefits.

- **Yellow beeswax** can still be used for candles, but will not showcase the colors in the mica powder as well as a white beeswax base will. White beeswax is typically chosen for aesthetic reasons.

Both yellow and white beeswax can be used for creating holistic products such as lip balms, lotions, soaps and as previously mentioned, candles. Again, before choosing a beeswax product be sure it is authentic and does not contain filler ingredients.

Bentonite clay

Bentonite clay is also known as montmorillonite clay and is formed from volcanic ash. Most of today's current harvesting of bentonite clay is done in Fort Benton, Wyoming, where large amounts of volcanos can be found. This clay has been used since ancient times as a natural, detoxifying agent. Bentonite clay contains minerals. It naturally contains calcium, magnesium, silica, sodium, copper, iron, and potassium. Ancient cultures used it as a dietary supplement since the clay is a natural source of important minerals.

Body butters

Body butters are a luxurious comfort item that not only moisturize the skin but also enrich it with vitamins and nutrients. Thicker than lotions, they promote wellness for the skin and can help your skin look younger and can reduce the look of fine lines and wrinkles.

To properly use these amazing substances, you first want to make sure your skin is clean and primed to soak in the most nutrients possible. Exfoliating your skin by dry brushing or using a salt or sugar scrub before applying body butter preps your pores to absorb the healing ingredients. Another way to promote the healing benefits of body butters is to apply them after you bathe or shower. When the skin is moist and clean, it can further absorb nutrients.

It is important to choose a high-quality body butter product that does not contain any unnatural ingredients or fillers.

There are multiple natural body butters that are available such as mango, shea, jojoba, and cocoa butter.

Borax

Borax occurs naturally in salt deposits in California's Death Valley. Naturally occurring borax is refined by a process of recrystallization but can also be produced synthetically from other boron compounds. Borax is used in a variety of household items such as laundry and cleaning products.

Carrier oil

Carrier oils are widely used to dilute essential oils and other organic compounds before they are applied to the skin or used in alternative therapy modalities. They are named carrier oils because they "carry" the essential oil or other organic item into the skin. Using carrier oils is a common safety practice when using essential oils for holistic health purposes.

Popular carrier oils:

Almond oil
Apricot oil
Avocado oil
Castor oil
Grapeseed oil
Jojoba Oil
Olive Oil
Pomegranate Seed oil
Sweet Almond Oil

Castile soap

Originally created in Castile, Spain, this soap is created with holistic ingredients such as olive and a variety of other oils, all of which can be derived from plant, nut, or vegetables sources. It is used as a natural base for many holistic products such as laundry detergents, shampoos, soaps, and hygiene products.

Castor oil

Castor oil is a substance extracted from the seeds of the Ricinus communis plant. Castor beans contain ricin, which is a toxic enzyme that loses its toxic properties when it is processed through high temperatures. Castor oil, in its processed form is used for many alternative remedies. It can be a great natural solution for many haircare concerns. It can be used as a natural hair conditioner and can also be used to heal a dry, flakey scalp and reduce dandruff. It has also been shown to increase hair growth in some people and is used to naturally combat hair loss.

Castor oil contains ricinoleic acid, which is a fatty acid in castor oil that stimulates a laxative effect in the intestines, therefore inducing bowel movements. It has natural antimicrobial properties, which are useful in the treatment and prevention of acne breakouts. It has also been shown to be a safe natural treatment for skin conditions such as psoriasis and eczema.

Epsom salt

Epsom salt gets its name because it was first discovered in Surrey, England. It is comprised of magnesium, sulfur, and oxygen. It is a common base in holistic comfort products such as bath bombs. It can also be used in gardening and can be used to naturally alleviate muscle soreness when added to warm bath soaks.

Essential Oils

Essential oils are compounds derived from plants, flowers, herbs, and fruits that can be used for medical, culinary and comfort purposes. They are used to treat physical, emotional, and psychological ailments and promote general well-being. The use of essential oils is widely practiced in holistic and alternative medicine.

Ways to use Essential Oils

- Aromatherapy- Using essential oils in a diffuser is a great way to promote wellness and improve the air quality in your home, car, or office. Diffused essential oils can be used to treat a wide variety of issue such as: reducing anxiety, creating focus, or increasing libido just to name a few! Aromatherapy has been scientifically proven to trigger your olfactory senses, which can improve circulation, help you feel   and improve your general feeling of wellness.

- Application- Applying essential oils to tense or painful areas or using products such as creams or soaps infused with your choice blend is a great way to enjoy the benefits of various oils. Many holistic practitioners and massage therapists apply essential oils to pressure points during treatment; creating a healing effect for their patients.

- Bathing- Soaking in essential oils is a great way to achieve maximum benefits from the natural healing power of various herbs, flowers, and plants! There are many wonderful products such as essential oil infused bath bombs, soaks and body washes that can help you incorporate better wellness in your personal hygiene.

- Compression- Essential oils added to a warm, wet washcloth can be used as a compress when applied to painful or swollen areas of the body. Essential oil compresses have been widely used to treat menstrual cramps, tense muscles, headaches, and post-exercise soreness.

Benefits of Using Essential Oils

There are hundreds of essential oil options, blends, and remedies for just about every ailment. A holistic health practitioner or licensed aromatherapist can help guide you to oils to improve your well-being. Essential oils can be applied in various different ways and some can even be taken internally for medicinal purposes.

Cautions about Using Essential Oils

Do not ingest any essential oil without first checking with your physician, as some essential oils can interact with medications or certain conditions. Be sure you are using a bio-friendly, 100% therapeutic grade oil. Do not ingest or diffuse low-quality oils, as they may be filled with other products and not 100% pure. You will not get adequate health benefits from a fake oil.

Felts Naptha

Fels-Naptha soap was originally created in 1893 by Fels and Company. It is an American brand of laundry soap used for pre-treating clothing stains and as a home remedy for poison ivy and other skin issues.

Glycerin

Glycerin also referred to as vegetable glycerin, glycerol, or glycerine, is a transparent liquid which can be derived from coconut, soybean or palm oils. It is a widely used ingredient in many hygiene products such as: lotions and deodorants. It is also used as a base to create herbal tinctures.

Kosher salt

Kosher salt is used as an ingredient in many holistic homemaking recipes. For example, it can be used to clean cast iron cookware. It can be used as an alternative to cleaning chemicals such as calcium carbonate. Kosher salt is also used for culinary purposes and is preferred in some diets over traditional table salt because it does not contain iodine.

Mica

Mica is a color additive powder obtained from the naturally occurring mineral, muscovite mica which contains potassium aluminum silicate. Currently, there is no definition or regulation to differentiate between natural and synthetic mica powder though synthetic mica must still contain FDA approved color additives to be considered cosmetic grade. This powder is used to add color to many holistic products such as makeup items, bath soaks and homemade candles.

Neem

Neem oil is produced by cold pressing the fruit and seeds of the neem oil tree, azadirachta indica. Neem oil has a green-brown or dark brown color that has a pungent garlic like aroma. Neem oil's main component is azadirachtin, which gives the oil its antiseptic, antifungal, antipyretic and antihistamine properties. It is an antiseptic and anti-fungal in nature that takes care of our overall health. Pure neem oil is loaded with fatty acids and alkaloids.

Neem can naturally protect outdoor animals such as horses from biting flies and mosquitos. Cats, dogs and hamsters can find relief from flea and mite bites as well. A diluted neem oil solution can be used as a natural soap or shampoo for pets to keep fleas, ticks, and mites away from your furry friends. It is safe for both indoor and outdoor pets. It can also be safely used to prevent insects in your garden. Neem is a great holistic alternative to dangerous pesticides. It is safe to use around plants and will not kill them, it will however, slowly decrease the amount of pests in your garden.

Unflavored gelatin

Unflavored gelatin is also known as granular gelatin. It is made from animal collagen which is a protein derived from cartilage, bones, skin, connective tissues and tendons. It can be used to create natural products such as air freshener and jelly soaps. However, this ingredient is not vegan due to it being derived from animal sources.

Vinegar

Vinegar is a liquid solution comprised of acetic acid and trace chemical created by the fermentation of ethanol or sugars by acetic acid bacteria. It is a common ingredient in many holistic cleaning recipes.

Witch Hazel

Witch hazel, scientifically known as Hamamelis virginiana is native to North America and is widely used for naturopathic and alternative remedies. It is a staple in natural first aid kits because of its antiseptic properties. It can be used to clean scrapes and wounds in the place of isopropyl alcohol or hydrogen peroxide.

Chapter 3: Holistic Homemaking Recipes

Air Freshener Spray

Ingredients
- 1 Large Glass Spray Bottle
- 1/2 Cup Water
- 2/3 Cup Witch Hazel
- 10 drops Essential Oil of Choice

Instructions
1. Add water and witch hazel into spray bottle.
2. Shake until combined.
3. Add 10 drops of essential oil of choice
4. Shake vigorously until blended.
5. Label the bottle and place in a cool place away from kids and pets.
6. To Use: Spray as desired to naturally freshen and disinfect the air.

Bathroom Cleaner

Ingredients
- 2 Cups Water
- 1/3 Cup Castile Soap
- 20 drops Lemon Essential Oil
- 15 drops Tea Tree Essential Oil
- Large Glass Spray Bottle

Instructions
1. Warm the water in microwave or stove top until it is hot but not boiling.
2. Add 1/3 cup of castile soap
3. Add 20 drops of lemon essential oil.
4. Add 15 drops of tea tree essential oil.
5. Stir until blended.
6. Carefully pour into spray bottle and shake gently to mix ingredients.
7. Be sure to label the container and store in a cool place away from kids and pets.
8. Use the mixture to disinfect and clean your bathroom without toxic chemicals.

Dishwasher Pods

Ingredients
- 20 drops Lemon Essential Oil
- 1/2 Cup Epsom Salt
- 2 Cups Baking Soda
- 2 Cups Borax
- 1/2 Cup Vinegar
- 1 Silicone Mold or Ice Cube tray

Instructions
1. Mix all dry ingredients except for vinegar into bowl.
2. Stir until mixture is blended.
3. Slowly and carefully pour in vinegar. (it is acidic and will cause a fizzy reaction and needs to be added very slowly.)
4. Stir mixture again until completely blended.
5. Carefully pack the mixture into the mold or ice cube tray. Pack it tightly so the mixture will form and harden.
6. For best results, let the mixture harden in a cool, dry place for 48 hours.
7. To Use: Place one tablet into your dishwasher to clean dishes.

Disinfectant Spray

Ingredients
- 1 Glass Spray Bottle
- 1/3 Cup Water
- 1/3 Cup Witch Hazel
- 10 Drops Tea Tree Essential Oil
- 10 Drops Clove Essential Oil
- 3 Sliced Lemons with Rinds

Instructions
1. Add water and witch hazel into spray bottle.
2. Shake until combined.
3. Add essential oils.
4. Shake Vigorously until blended.
5. Label the bottle and place in a cool place away from kids and pets.
6. To Use: Spray as desired to naturally freshen and disinfect the air.

Floor Cleaner

Ingredients
- 2 Cups Water
- 1 tablespoon Baking Soda
- 2 tablespoons Castile Soap
- 30 drops Tea Tree Essential Oil
- 20 drops Lemon Essential Oil
- 15 drops Orange Essential Oil
- 1 Glass Spray Bottle

Instructions
1. Warm the water on stove top until it is hot but not boiling.
2. Add 1 tablespoon of baking soda into the warm water, stir until dissolved.
3. Add 2 tablespoons of castile soap.
4. Add 30 drops of tea tree essential oil.
5. Add 20 drops of lemon essential oil.
6. Add 15 drops orange essential oil.
7. Stir until blended.
8. Carefully pour into spray bottle and shake gently to mix ingredients.
9. Be sure to label the container and store in a cool place away from kids and pets.
10. Use your natural cleaner to disinfect and clean your home without toxic chemicals!

Furniture Polish

Ingredients
- 1/2 Cup Olive Oil
- 25 Drops Orange Essential Oil
- 1-2 Orange Peels
- 1 Large Glass Spray Bottle

Instructions
1. Peel and slice 1-2 fresh oranges. Slice rind into small pieces and put into empty spray bottle.
2. Only put the orange peel into the mixture not the actual fruit as it will decay.
3. Pour 1/2 cup of Olive Oil into bottle.
4. Add 25 drops of orange essential oil into bottle.
5. Shake well to mix all ingredients.
6. Label the bottle and place in a cool area away from kids and pets.
7. To Use: Apply to dry cloth and wipe onto furniture to polish and dust naturally.

Gel Air Freshener

Ingredients
- Water
- 2 packs unflavored gelatin
- 1 tablespoons table salt
- 1-2 teaspoons essential oil of choice
- Small Glass container (Little mason jars work well for this recipe)
- Seed sprouter lids
- Food coloring (Optional)

Instructions
1. Heat 3/4 cup water and 1 tablespoon of salt in a small saucepan.
2. Slowly add the gelatin and stir until completely dissolved.
3. Remove from heat.
4. Add 1/4 cup water.
5. Carefully pour into the mason jars
6. Add up to 1 teaspoon of essential oil of choice into jars (Optional- Add food coloring of choice)
7. Add seed starter lid to jar lid.
8. Allow to cool for 12 hours.
9. To use: Place in bathrooms or scent concerning areas for freshness.

Glass Cleaner

Ingredients
- ½ Cup White Vinegar
- ½ Distilled Water
- 5 Drops Lemon Essential Oil
- 1 Large Glass Spray Bottle

Instructions
1. Add the white vinegar to the spray bottle.
2. Pour 5 drops of lemon essential oil in the spray bottle.
3. Mix in the distilled water to the spray bottle.
4. Shake until all ingredients blend. (Spray will look cloudy.)
5. To use: Spray onto glass surfaces and wipe away with a paper towel for a streak free shine.

Laundry Detergent

Ingredients
- 1/3 Cup Kosher Salt
- 1/2 Felts Naptha Bar
- 15 drops of Essential Oil of Choice
- 1 cup Castile Soap
- 4 cups Water
- Heat resistant container which can be sealed

Instructions
1. Grate half the felts naptha bar into small shavings.
2. Heat 4 cups of water on stovetop.
3. Add felts naptha into heated water and stir until completely dissolved.
4. Once felts naptha is dissolved completely, add kosher salt.
5. Stir the mixture completely and remove from heat.
6. Add the castile soap, continue to stir.
7. *OPTIONAL* For a smoother consistency, you can put the mixture into a blender once it has cooled to a safe temperature but not gotten completely cooled.
8. Once you have blended the ingredients, add the desired essential oils into the mixture.
9. Store in an air sealed container, as the detergent will dry out if left open.
10. Be sure to store safely away from children and pets.

Surface Disinfectant Wipes Recipe

Ingredients
- 1 roll of paper towels
- 1/4 cup of isopropyl alcohol
- 1/3 cup water
- 10 drops of lemon essential oil
- 10 drops of orange essential oil
- 10 drops of clove essential oil
- Soaking basin such as a sealed bowl with lid.

Instructions
1. Purchase a high-quality paper towel product.
2. Cut paper towel roll in half.
3. Pour water, isopropyl alcohol and clove, lemon and orange essential oils into soaking basin.
4. Mix thoroughly.
5. Add ½ paper towel roll into soaking basin.
6. Immerse ½ paper towel roll in mixture completely.
7. Store in an airtight container in a cool, safe place away from kids and pets.
8. To Use: Use one sheet of paper towel to disinfect surfaces.
9. Be careful to avoid getting into eyes, mouth and open wounds/cuts when using the wipes.

Chapter 4: Personal Hygiene Recipes

Acne Cleansing Mask

Ingredients
- 3 Tablespoons Bentonite Clay
- 1 Tablespoon Activated Charcoal
- 3 Tablespoons Witch Hazel
- 10 drops Lavender Essential Oil

Instructions
1. Mix the bentonite clay and the activated charcoal.
2. Pour in Witch Hazel.
3. Add 10 drops lavender essential oil.
4. Stir until all ingredients are blended.
5. To Use: Carefully apply the facial mask and do not get mixture into your eyes or mouth.
6. Let the mask dry and keep on skin for 15 minutes.
7. Rinse the mask off thoroughly with cold water.
8. Label and store remaining mixture in an airtight container away from kids and pets.

Acne Astringent

Ingredients
- 1/3 Cup of Witch Hazel
- 5 drops Lemon Essential Oil
- 3 drops Frankincense Essential Oil
- Glass container

Instructions
1. Pour 1/3 cup of Witch Hazel into a glass container.
2. Mix in lemon, frankincense essential oils
3. Shake well.
4. To use: Wash face. Apply a quarter sized amount of mixture to a cotton ball or clean washcloth and apply to face. Let mixture set on skin for 3-5 minutes before rinsing with cool water.

Naturally Moisturizing Conditioner

Ingredients
- 4 tablespoons Mayonnaise
- 2/3 Cup Shea Butter
- 12 Drops Lavender Essential Oil

Instructions

1. Heat the shea butter in microwave or stove top on medium/warm until it becomes liquid.
2. Add 4 tablespoons of mayonnaise.
3. Add 12 Drops of Lavender Essential Oil.
4. Stir until mixture is combined.
5. Cover in airtight container and let mixture rest for 2-4 hours.
6. To Use: After shampooing, apply a palm sized amount to split ends for 10 minutes for a deep conditioning treatment. Rinse completely and let hair air dry for best results.

Holistic Shampoo

Ingredients
- 1/3 cup Distilled Water
- 1/4 cup Castile Soap
- 1 Teaspoon Vegetable Glycerin
- 5 drops of Essential oil of choice (Be sure to choose a skin safe essential oil)

Instructions
1. Pour 1/3 cup of water and castile soap into a glass container.
2. Mix in essential oil of choice and glycerin.
3. Shake well until all ingredients are blended completely.
4. To Use: Apply to wet hair and lather, scrubbing mixture gently into scalp. Rinse thoroughly and repeat as desired.

Skin Disinfecting Wipes

Ingredients
- 1/3 cup Distilled Water
- 10 tablespoons of Witch Hazel
- 5 drops of tea tree essential oil
- 5 drops of rosemary essential oil

Instructions
1. Purchase a high-quality paper towel product.
2. Cut paper towel roll in half.
3. Pour water, witch hazel and add tea tree and rosemary essential oils into soaking basin.
4. Mix thoroughly.
5. Add ½ paper towel roll into soaking basin.
6. Immerse ½ paper towel roll in mixture completely.
7. Store in an airtight container in a cool, safe place away from kids and pets.

Tooth Whitening Paste

Ingredients
- 1/2 Teaspoon <u>Activated Charcoal</u>
- 2 Tablespoons Baking Soda
- 2 Tablespoons Coconut Oil
- 1 Saucepan
- Airtight Glass Container

Instructions
1. Melt the coconut oil in a small saucepan on medium heat.
2. Once melted, pour into a heat resistant bowl and add in the activated charcoal and baking soda.
3. Stir mixture until it is cool enough to pour into glass, airtight container.
4. To Use: Dip toothbrush into mixture and brush teeth liberally.
5. Be sure to rinse your mouth completely after use and do not swallow the mixture.

Chapter 5: Miscellaneous Recipes

Ant Repellent

Ingredients
- 1 Glass Spray Bottle
- 25 Drops Clove Essential Oil
- 20 Drops Tea Tree Essential Oil
- 15 Drops Peppermint Essential Oil
- 2/3 Cup Water

Instructions
1. Add water into spray bottle.
2. Add 25 drops Clove essential oil.
3. Add 20 drops Tea Tree Essential Oil.
4. Add 15 drops Peppermint Essential Oil.
5. Shake until blended.
6. Label the bottle and place in a safe, cool place away from kids and pets.
7. To Use: Spray around ant infested areas to repel insects.

Anti-Flea Pet Rinse

Ingredients
- 1 Glass Bottle
- 1/3 cup Jojoba Oil
- 3 teaspoons Neem Oil

Instructions
1. Pour jojoba oil into empty bottle.
2. Add 3 teaspoons of Neem Oil.
3. Shake well until mixture is blended.
4. Label and store in a cool dry place away from kids and pets.
5. To Use: Thoroughly apply to your pet, covering their coat completely. Let set 15 minutes. Rinse the animal well. May repeat up to 3x weekly as needed for flea and tick control.

Baby Wipes

Ingredients
- 1/3 cup distilled water
- 4 tablespoons of mineral oil
- 5 tablespoons of castile soap

Instructions
8. Purchase a high-quality paper towel product.
9. Cut paper towel roll in half.
10. Pour water, witch hazel and mineral oil and castile soap into soaking basin.
11. Mix thoroughly.
12. Add ½ paper towel roll into soaking basin.
13. Immerse ½ paper towel roll in mixture completely.
14. Store in an airtight container in a cool, safe place away from kids and pets.

Bug Repellent

Ingredients
- 1 Glass Spray Bottle
- 1/2 Water
- 10 Teaspoons Witch Hazel
- 20 drops Lemongrass Essential Oil

Instructions
1. Add water and witch hazel into spray bottle.
2. Add 10 drops of lemongrass essential oil.
3. Shake vigorously until blended.
4. To Use: Spray onto body before outdoor activity to repel insects.

Eyelash Growth Serum

Ingredients
- 1 Teaspoon Almond Oil
- 1 Teaspoon Vitamin E Oil
- 1 Teaspoon Castor Oil
- Glass Container

Instructions

1. Add vitamin E oil, almond oil and castor in into a bowl.
2. Stir all ingredients are completely blended.
3. Pour mixture into empty mascara applicator using a tiny funnel, medicine dropper or small spoon.
4. To Use: Apply to lashes nightly to promote natural lash stimulation.
5. Do not get this mixture in your eyes only apply to lashes.

Jelly Soap

Ingredients
- 1 packet Unflavored Gelatin
- 1/2 Cup Body Wash of Choice or Natural Liquid Soap Base
- 1 Cup Cold Water
- 1 Saucepan
- 1 Measuring Cup
- 1 Silicone Mold
- *Optional* 2 tsp Natural Food Colorant

Instructions
1. Add 1 packet of unflavored gelatin into cup of cold water.
2. Pour gelatin water into saucepan and place it on the burner using the medium heat setting.
3. Stir until fully melted for 5 mins.
4. Pour into bowl while still warm, mix with body wash and stir.
5. *Optional* Add natural food coloring.
6. When mixture is completely stirred, carefully pour into mold.
7. Place in fridge for 6-8 hours.
8. Once mixture has set, carefully remove from mold.
9. To Use: Lather soap onto skin, rinse and repeat as desired.

Mascara

Ingredients
- 1 Empty Mascara Tube
- 2 Teaspoons Activated Charcoal
- 1/2 Teaspoon Bentonite Clay
- 3 Teaspoons Vegetable Glycerin
- 1 Teaspoon Aloe Vera gel

Instructions

1. Mix 3 teaspoons of vegetable glycerin and 1 teaspoon of aloe vera gel into mixing bowl.
2. Slowly sprinkle in bentonite clay and activated charcoal.
3. Stir until completely blended until all clumps of clay have dissolved.
4. Carefully pour into mascara tube.
5. To use: Apply to lashes, careful to not get mascara in your eyes.

Pet Calming Spray

Ingredients
- 1 Spray Bottle
- 10 drops Lavender Essential Oil
- 5 Drops Lemongrass Essential Oil
- 2/3 cup warm water

Instructions
1. Fill spray bottle with warm water.
2. Add 10 drops of lavender essential oil
3. Add 5 drops of lemongrass essential oil
4. Shake mixture until all ingredients are blended.
5. To Use: Gently spray on your pets, careful to avoid their eyes.

Sleepy time salve

Ingredients
- 15 Tablespoons Carrier Oil of Choice
- 10 Drops Chamomile Essential Oil
- 5 Drops Lavender Essential Oil
- 2 Drops Rose Essential Oil
- 1 Empty Glass Bottle

Instructions
1. Pour 15 Tablespoons of Jojoba carrier oil into empty bottle.
2. Add 10 Drops Chamomile Essential Oil.
3. Add 5 Drops Lavender Essential Oil.
4. Add 2 drops Rose Essential Oil.
5. Shake well until ingredients are fully blended.
6. To Use: Apply to skin one hour before bedtime for relaxation.

Weedkiller

Ingredients
- ½ Gallon White Vinegar
- ¼ Cup Lemon Juice
- ½ cup Castile Soap
- ½ cup Epson salt

Instructions
1. In a large bucket placed in a well-ventilated area, pour white vinegar, castile soap and Epson salt into the bucket.
2. Stir those ingredients until blended.
3. Add lemon juice.
4. Stir mixture and use immediately.
5. Do not store these mixed ingredients together and use complete mixture on lawn.
6. To Use: Spray on weed ridden areas on your lawn.

Chapter 6: First Aid Kit Recipes

Antiseptic Spray

Ingredients
- Glass Spray Bottle
- 5 teaspoons Isopropyl alcohol
- 10 teaspoons Witch Hazel
- 10 drops Lemon essential oil

Instructions
1. Clean spray bottle and dry thoroughly.
2. Pour alcohol, witch hazel and lemon essential oil into spray bottle.
3. Shake until all ingredients are mixed.
4. To Use: Spray onto hands and rub until dry.

Congestion Relief Rub

Ingredients
- 1/4 Cup Shea Butter
- 1/4 Cup Carrier Oil of Choice
- 1 Teaspoon Beeswax
- 10 Drops Peppermint Essential Oil
- 10 Drops Lemon Essential Oil
- 5 Drops Eucalyptus Essential Oil
- 1 Saucepan
- 1 Heat Resistant Container (Such as Mason Jar)

Instructions

1. Fill saucepan halfway full with water and set to medium heat until warm.
2. Add beeswax, shea butter and almond oil into double boiler.
3. Let ingredients melt, stir as needed until blended fully.
4. Remove from heat once melted.
5. Stir and allow mixture to cool but still remain warm.
6. Add the essential oils.
7. Stir and allow mixture to cool slightly before transferring to empty container.
8. Pour mixture into empty container.
9. Label and store in a safe, cool place away from kids and pets.
10. To Use: Apply a liberal amount to your chest as needed for congestion relief.

Pain Relief Rub

Ingredients
- 15 Tablespoons Carrier Oil of Choice
- 10 Drops Tea Tree Essential Oil
- 5 Drops Eucalyptus Essential Oil
- 5 Drops Peppermint Essential Oil
- 1 Empty Glass Bottle

Instructions
1. Pour 15 tablespoons of carrier oil into empty bottle.
2. Add 10 drops Tea Tree Essential Oil.
3. Add 5 drops Eucalyptus Essential Oil.
4. Add 5 drops Peppermint Essential Oil.
5. Shake well until ingredients are fully blended.
6. To Use: Apply to sore muscles and joints after a workout for natural soreness relief.

Restless Leg Relief Rub

Ingredients
- 1/2 Cup Magnesium Oil
- 1 Empty Spray Bottle
- 15 Drops Peppermint Essential Oil
- 10 Drops Lavender Essential Oil
- 1/4 Cup Water

Instructions
1. Pour water into empty bottle.
2. Add 15 Drops of Peppermint Essential Oil.
3. Add 10 Drops of Lavender Essential Oil.
4. Carefully pour in magnesium oil.
5. *Note* It will not completely blend within the water so be sure to shake the mixture before use.
6. Shake until blended.
7. To use: Spray onto legs and massage gently to soothe restless legs and cramping before bedtime.

Cautions Magnesium oil can be sedating, especially when paired with lavender essential oil. Do not use if you are driving and need to be attentive. Do not start or stop any medical treatment without first contacting your healthcare provider. Magnesium can interact with certain medications and can have contraindications in those with kidney disease.

Stretch Mark Salve

Ingredients
- 1/2 Cup Shea Butter
- 10 Teaspoons Vitamin E Oil
- 1 Teaspoon of Beeswax
- 10 Drops Rose Essential Oil
- 5 Drops Frankincense Essential Oil
- 1 Saucepan
- 1 Empty Container
- 1 Heat Resistant Container (Such as Mason Jar)

Instructions
1. Fill saucepan halfway full with water and set to medium/high heat until boiling.
2. Add beeswax, shea butter and Vitamin E oil into heat resistant container (such as mason jar) and place into saucepan.
3. Let ingredients melt, stir as needed until blended fully.
4. Remove from heat once melted.
5. Stir and allow mixture to cool but still remain warm.
6. Add the essential oils.
7. Stir and allow mixture to cool slightly before transferring to empty container.
8. Pour mixture into empty container.
9. Label and store in a safe, cool place away from kids and pets.
10. To Use: Apply liberally to stretch marks and let soak into skin.

Sunscreen

Ingredients
- 1/4 Cup Fractionated Coconut Oil
- 2 Tablespoons Zinc Oxide
- 1 Tablespoon Vitamin E oil
- 2 Tablespoons Shea butter
- 1 Teaspoon Beeswax
- 1/2 Cup Olive Oil
- 1 Heat Resistant Container (such as mason jar)
- 1 Saucepan

Instructions

1. Put saucepan halfway filled with water on stovetop.
2. Add all ingredients except zinc oxide into another smaller saucepan.
3. Place smaller saucepan into water filled saucepan and turn burner on medium heat.
4. Once water is hot but not boiling, stir until the ingredients are fully melted and combined.
5. Remove mixture from warm water and add in the zinc oxide.
6. Stir until completely blended and allow to cool before use.
7. To Use: Apply liberally to skin prior to sun exposure.

Natural "Neosporin"

Ingredients
- 1/4 Cup Shea Butter
- 1/4 Cup Almond Oil
- 1 Teaspoon Beeswax
- 10 Drops Tea Tree Essential Oil
- 10 Drops Lemon Essential Oil
- 5 Drops Frankincense Essential Oil
- 1 Saucepan
- 1 Heat Resistant Container (Such as Mason Jar)

Instructions
1. Put saucepan halfway filled with water on stovetop.
2. Add all ingredients except essential oils into another smaller saucepan.
3. Place smaller saucepan into water filled saucepan and turn burner on medium heat.
4. Once water is hot but not boiling, stir until the ingredients are fully melted and combined.
5. Remove from heat once melted.
6. Stir and allow mixture to cool but still remain warm.
7. Add essential oils.
8. Stir and allow mixture to cool slightly before transferring out of saucepan.
9. Pour mixture into heat resistant container.
10. Label and store in a safe, cool place away from kids and pets.
11. To Use: Apply a quarter sized amount to wounds to naturally promote antibacterial healing. For best results, clean wound with peroxide then apply the natural salve and cover with bandage.

Chapter 7: Comfort Products

Anti-Anxiety Calming Wipe Recipe

Ingredients
- 1 roll of paper towels
- 10 drops of Lavender essential oil
- 5 drops of Chamomile essential oil
- 3 tablespoons of mineral oil
- ¼ cup water
- Soaking basin such as a sealed bowl with lid.

Instruction
1. Cut paper towel roll in half.
2. Pour water, mineral oil and essential oils into soaking basin.
3. Mix thoroughly.
4. Add ½ paper towel roll into soaking basin.
5. Immerse ½ paper towel roll in mixture completely.
6. Store in an airtight container in a cool, safe place away from kids and pets.

Bath Bombs (Citric Acid Free)

Ingredients
- ½ Cup Baking Soda
- 2 Cups Epson Salt
- ½ Cup Cream of Tartar
- Essential Oil of Choice
- Flexible Mold
- Spray bottle filled with distilled water
- Whisk
- *Optional* 1 teaspoon mica powder for coloring

Instruction
1. Pour baking soda, Epsom salt and cream of tartar into mixing bowl.
2. Mix thoroughly with whisk.
3. Add essential oils and mica powder.
4. Stir mixture completely.
5. Spray flexible mold lightly with water.
6. Pack mixture into mold tightly.
7. Lightly spray the top of the mixture in the mold with water to set it.
8. Allow to set for 24 hours before carefully removing from mold.
9. To Use: Drop into warm bathwater and let dissolve for a comforting natural bath bomb experience.

Lemon Shea Butter Soap

Ingredients
- 2/3 cup Shea Butter
- 20 Drops lemon essential oil
- 6 oz glycerin soap base
- Saucepan
- *Optional* 1 teaspoon yellow mica powder

Instructions
1. Place the glycerin soap in saucepan on stovetop and melt slowly on low heat.
2. Stir until mixture is completely melted.
3. Slowly add shea butter and stir until melted.
4. Add 20 drops of lemon essential oil and food colorant.
5. Stir until smooth.
6. Pour the soap mixture into the silicone molds and set aside to cool for 24 hours.
7. After 24 hours, remove soap from the mold and
8. Store in an airtight container to prevent them from drying out.
9. To Use: Apply to skin during bathing for hygiene.

Spiced Apple Body Butter

Ingredients
- 20 Teaspoons Cocoa Butter
- 1 Teaspoon Apple Cider Vinegar
- 1 Teaspoon Natural Vanilla Extract
- 1 Saucepan
- 1 Empty Lotion Container

Instructions
1. Put saucepan halfway filled with water on stovetop.
2. Add all ingredients except vanilla extract into another smaller saucepan.
3. Place smaller saucepan into water filled saucepan and turn burner on medium heat.
4. Once water is hot but not boiling, stir until the ingredients are fully melted and combined.
5. Remove from heat once melted.
6. Add natural vanilla extract.
7. Stir mixture until it is cooled but still warm.
8. Carefully pour mixture into heat resistant container.
9. Allow to cool 2 hours before use.
10. Label and store away from kids or pets.
11. To Use: Apply to body to naturally moisturize your skin with a fresh, fall scent.

Chapter 9: Conclusion

Holistic health can be a wonderful way to take control of your toxic exposure. You are truly in control of what products you clean your home with, what food you put into your body and what products you allow on your skin.

You can take control of your chemical exposure by practicing the "Three R's."

- **Read**
- **Research**
- **Replace**

1. Read every label of every product that you purchase.
2. Research the ingredients found in the products.
3. Replace concerning products with natural, nontoxic solutions.

This is your life; you owe it to yourself to live the very best one possible.

References

1. Landrigan PJ, Carlson JE. Environmental policy and children's health. Future Child. 1995 Summer-Fall;5(2):34-52. PMID: 8528687.

2. Some candles with lead wicks emit lead into the air. (n.d.). University of Michigan News and Information Services http://ns.umich.edu/Releases/1999/Oct99/r100699.html

3. University of Washington (2010, October 28). Scented consumer products shown to emit many unlisted chemicals. https://www.washington.edu/news/2010/10/28/scented-consumer-products-shown-to-emit-many-unlisted-chemicals-3/

4. Environment International, Volume 86, 2016, Pages 45-51, ISSN 0160-4120

5. University of Washington. (2010, October 28). Scented consumer products shown to emit many unlisted chemicals. https://www.washington.edu/news/2010/10/28/scented-consumer-products-shown-to-emit-many-unlisted-chemicals-3/

6. Environmental Protection Agency. (n.d.). 1,4-Dioxane (1,4-Diethyleneoxide). Retrieved from https://www.epa.gov/assessing-and-managing-chemicals-under-tsca/risk-evaluation-14-dioxane

7. James MO, Li W, Summerlot DP, Rowland-Faux L, Wood CE. Triclosan is a potent inhibitor of estradiol and estrone sulfonation in sheep placenta. Environ Int. 2010 Nov;36(8):942-9. doi: 10.1016/j.envint.2009.02.004. Epub 2009 Mar 18. PMID: 19299018; PMCID: PMC4789100.

8. Diethanolamine [Https://monographs.iarc.who.int/wp-content/uploads/2018/06/mono101-004.pdf]. (n.d.).

9. Breast Cancer Prevention Partners. (n.d.). Parabens. Retrieved from https://www.bcpp.org/resource/parabens/

10. Drug Bank (n.d.). Aluminum chlorohydrate. Retrieved from https://go.drugbank.com/drugs/DB11573

Acknowledgements

This book was sponsored by Hope, Healing, Happy Co.

A holistic company established to help others find hope, healing and happiness in mind, body and spirit through natural products, self-help books, chronic illness lifestyle management, holistic health coaching and educational seminars to help clients improve their quality of life.

For more information, great DIY recipes and also resources on living a holistic lifestyle, visit **hopehealinghappy.com**

About the Author

Winslow E. Dixon was a driven healthcare professional in the field of geriatrics who was pursuing a medical degree, but upon her devastating dual diagnosis of Medullary Sponge Kidney and Addison's Disease, Winslow was forced to find a new purpose when her health changed her destiny.

She is now a published author, freelance writer and columnist. She volunteers her time as an advocate for those suffering with chronic illnesses, rare diseases and disabilities as the CEO of Adrenal Alternatives Foundation.

She is the author of the fiction series: Townsend the EverVigilant Series and the books: Cortisol Pump 101: A Patient's Guide to the Cortisol Pumping Method , Adrenal Insufficiency 101: A Patient's Guide to Managing Adrenal Insufficiency the Arsenal of Arrows Devotional Journal Challenge Series, the Peace by Piece 365 Inspirational Health Log Journal the children's book The Shivering Sunbeam which explains disability in a way young minds can understand and Chronically Stoned: The Guide to Winning the Battle against Kidney Stones and UTI's. She has also published many articles on reputable websites such as Yahoo News, Yahoo Lifestyle and the Mighty. Her poetry work has also been featured in many publications such as the Emerging American Writers Anthology and Florida's Emerging Poets.

She is a motivational speaker and has dedicated her life to spreading hope. She also works in natural health and helps her clients achieve better quality of life through the holistic business, Hope Healing Happy Co.

Winslow lives by her motto:

"Your fairytales may turn into nightmares, but you can still slay dragons." ©

More information can be found at the links:
Winslow's website: **winslowedixon.wordpress.com**
Townsend: EverVigilant Series website: **townsendseries.com**

Upcoming publications in the Holistic Homemaking Series:
Bath Soaks for Better Health
Children's Holistic Recipe Collection
Diffuser Blend Recipe Collection
DIY Gifts Recipe Collection
Explaining Essential Oils
Guide to Aromatherapy
Guide to Herbal Teas
Guide to Natural Detoxification
Guide to Natural Lifestyle Modifications
Holiday Recipe Collection
Holistic Help: Natural Anxiety Relief
Holistic Help: Natural Energy Boosters
Holistic Help: Natural First Aid Solutions
Holistic Help: Natural Immune Boosters
Holistic Help: Natural Pain Relief Solutions
Holistic Help: Natural Stress Relief
Men's Holistic Recipe Collection
Pet's Holistic Recipe Collection
Women's Holistic Recipe Collection

Wishing you hope, healing & happiness.
Thank you for reading <u>Holistic Homemaking.</u>

Sincerely,
Author Winslow E. Dixon

www.ingramcontent.com/pod-product-compliance
Lightning Source LLC
Chambersburg PA
CBHW070800050426
42452CB00012B/2421